I0223846

# She Lives There Still

*Also by Mary Leader*

Red Signature
The Penultimate Suitor
Beyond the Fire

# Mary Leader

# She Lives There Still

Shearsman Books

First published in the United Kingdom in 2018 by
Shearsman Books
50 Westons Hill Drive
Emersons Green
BRISTOL
BS16 7DF

Shearsman Books Ltd Registered Office
30–31 St. James Place, Mangotsfield, Bristol BS16 9JB
*(this address not for correspondence)*

www.shearsman.com

ISBN 978-1-84861-584-7

Copyright © Mary Leader, 2018.
The right of Mary Leader to be identified as the author
of this work has been asserted by her in accordance with the
Copyrights, Designs and Patents Act of 1988.
All rights reserved.

ACKNOWLEDGMENTS
*Antioch Review*: 'My mind, maybe call it temperament, saw'

*Cimarron Review*: 'Fall, when optimism rolls out a grand'

*The Laurel Review*: 'You gave a talk. I asked if you'd send me'; 'Bewildered, me.
Why would Leibniz's wig'; 'International Luminary, you.'

*Notre Dame Review*: 'At the border, all couriers are searched'; 'For her, not
anymore, no trying out'; 'Where Spring blows in, not to emptied-out air'

*The Quarterly*: 'A Coastal Story'

*Shearsman*: 'And, well, should she rule for mythology'; 'Encounters in the
Abyss'; 'Icarus, whose myth, as parsed by her muse'; 'Listening Man'; 'Peggy
married a rich man named Hayden'; 'She accepts sere July. She may as well';
'She sleeps. Near her sleep tame animals. Not''; 'Sleep, she has learned, is both
collective and'; 'When, from profundity, comes forth thunder'

An earlier version of 'An Inland Story' (titled 'In November') appeared in
*A Festschrift for Tony Frazer*, 2015.

This book, in genesis and in execution, would not exist but for deep assistance
and years of inspiration from Sara Leader, Edward Leader, Donald Platt,
and Dana Roeser.

# Contents

for Arlene Joan Johnson

*There was an old woman*
*Lived under a hill;*
*And if she's not gone,*
*She lives there still.*

—Mother Goose

## A Coastal Story

My heart is not in her room.
   Look. Her bed is made up, and she is gone.

From the attic window, I spot her
     at dawn, at sea,
  a delicate skiff, journeyed by wind, upon a dissolving
       surface.

She left a note:
    *I love him, I love him, that's all*
  a girl so used to
      her chin in her hand, her studious lamp.

What happens next? what next? I don't know!
   And neither, goddamn him, does he.

# A Pregnancy of Titles

*Crone Cards*
*Last Love*
*Possible Esoterica*

*Possible Love*
*Possible Cards*
*Crone Love*

*Crone Esoterica*
*Last Cards*
*Last Esoterica*

# A Warty Chin

*Stranger.* . . . taking on the one hand those whose natures tend rather to courage, which is the stronger element and may be regarded as the warp, and on the other hand those who incline to order and gentleness, and which are represented in the figure as spun thick and soft, after the manner of the woof—these, which are naturally opposed, she seeks to bind and weave together in the following manner:

*Young Socrates.* In what manner?

*Stranger.* First of all, she takes the eternal of the soul and binds it with a divine cord, to which it is akin, and then the animal nature, and binds that with human cords.

*Young Socrates.* I do not understand what you mean.

—Plato

## A

And, well, *should* she rule for mythology
versus history? What material
difference is there? Her eyes' irises, like
her heaped years, contain flecks, demarcations,
unlike lead, unlike gold, more like jasper.
In her scales, she keeps bark-dust. She plies yarns.
She dreams a falcon, bark-dust in his hair.

What kind of society comes up with
sumptuary laws? Why limit cash spent
on food/drink/clothes/decor? Not that *she* can
afford dyes shipped from distant nation-states.
Though she's *read* of exotic reds, and blues,
"cochineal," and much forbidden "wode,"
herself, she goes in scorched shades and shades bleached.

## At

At the border, all *couriers* are searched.
Some *courtiers* are searched, whether they seek
love, position, faith. At the border, news
of public concern becomes clandestine,
while intimacy is forced to take place
in plain sight. Certain world-views will promote
the trek, the quest, the *con*quest. Weaponry:
predicate between crusader and ghost.

Other world-views will continue, no need
to promote, the hive, the hum, the sweet mead.
Midwifery: predicate between womb
and breath. Wool for covers ere there was silk.

Reprise, song. *When Í / get tó / the bór / dér*
—Richard Thompson, Muslim and Troubadour

# B

Bandannas show affection when people
tie them around their dogs' necks. Bandannas
add their touch to festivals, market days,
street fairs. Classic colors. Take red, take blue.
That small option makes even misanthropes,
with hearses for minds, express a preference.

Thanks to time, time going both ways, people
mount individual experiments.
Motivations behind, results after,
enter in, and yield, commonality.

These changes leave trails deep in the language.
"Bandanna" is derived from the Hindu.
"Lorry," from "lurry," *to pull*, meant not just
any draft horse, but one built large, and low.

# D

During the evening's first quartet, one girl
in the audience gestures toward applause
after the first movement, but catches on
in time that no one else is clapping yet.
At one point, her date, a music major,
whispers "pizzicato," miming a pluck.
One elderly husband dozes. His wife
glares at his immobile face. The girl nods
when music dude whispers "That's called droning
on an open string." The tag of the wife's
blouse sticks out. No one feels an embolism
slip mere millimeters. Players, beyond
the last note, let their bows hover, so as
not to impede the vibration's passing.

# E

Even when things are neither cold nor bleak,
if she goes for her walk, she takes her shawl.

She feels a kind of keen affection for
the small woodland creatures who cross the path,

or use the path. Yet nowhere can she find
the two children who had been in her charge,

a little girl and a little boy. True,
a full-grown woman and a full-grown man

bear the same names as those little children.
But these two know about mortality,

and are, at this time, more likely to cry
than she is. Their eyes brim of a sudden,

when she tries to speak with her ruined tongue,
when she tries to remember and does not.

F

Fantastic icicles hang from soffits
of a coaching inn, icicles figured
as harpies, suspended head-down, clear bats.

She is sure about that but cannot find
the book, frontispiece glazed by onionskin.

Gray tinges thin white curtains. Green tinges
gray sky, just such a sky as broods over
villagers, outdoor kettle, curl-tailed dogs,

Brueghel's *Hunters in the Snow*. How sharp, there,
the raven ciphers. In her trees, how sharp,
how teenage Goth black, the squirrel fingernails.

On sills are column candles, whose sides touch
the frigid mullions. Day-lit flames send up
rippled air, heat seen, not warmth felt. She turns.

## Fo

For her, not anymore, no trying out
ensues tomorrow, not for twirler, not
for cheerleader, not for first-chair flute, nor
does she ask other women how they plan
to thread up their needles. She knows. She sheds

company, seeks guild. She rummages out
antique brochures from Ely Cathedral,
picks from them things she would like to adapt
for bargello stitch eight hundred years on.
A needed knee pad. A misericord.

No madness bothers her. She's already
been abandoned. Her naps are like dust motes
in shallow recesses of old mines, where
not one speck of tin or copper remains.

## G–G a

Girly-Girl and Candide see that the old
broad is correct. It *is* dawn. Silhouette
light reveals her, "La Vieille's," profile; it
has a past. Her nose didn't *always* fold
over her lip, which turns blue as a cold
sun brings up color. She doesn't forget
to sugar the coffee, bless her petite
heart, but gives too much sage advice, once told

Girly-Girl, "Love him who is a *friend* to
you." Candide looked alarmed. Girly-Girl sauced
back, "Would but indulgent Fortune send *you*
a 'friend.'" Candide laughed. That hurt. But Old Broad
knew her forté. Theft. "Back to business, eh?
My mistress has *diamonds*. What do you say?"

## G-G g

Girly-Girl, guess what, ends up nicknamed "La
Vieille" herself. From her experience,
she thinks back to her theme. At least she tried.
Okay, she wasn't always very nice
to people but she wishes them well now.

*Let the girls do the gazing for a change,*
*and for another, let the boys reveal*
*desire gently, like ferns, not all the time,*
*not all the time, occasionally, though.*

She made every man jack of them want to
be in a couple, likewise every hen,
but in maturity, augments her spell.

*Let every couple make it through the night.*
*Let them wake up, decrepit, but to dew.*

## Gr

Grit shakes down into her low-sided shoes
on the way home from school. Phenomena
of season move with or without watching.

Maple seeds say grace then helicopter
to gravel, and off to the side, to mud,
to mud puddles, to float, briefly. Mornings,
she doesn't notice. Afternoons, she does.

An acorn may be kicked along in fall,
a pebble any time. In those jumpy
films of immigrants coming down ship-ramps
onto Ellis Island, the few old ones

know how to use a cane, the crook facing
forward, better angle for leverage.
With skill, they hobble, and with great purpose.

I

Icarus, whose myth, as parsed by her muse,
the polymath Arkady Plotnitsky,
"was particularly expressive from
this point of view: it split the sun in two:
the one that was shining at the moment
of the boy Icarus's elevation,
and the one that melted the wax causing
failure and a screaming fall when he got

too close." Her own myth, not written, phased moons
above a cliff-top Jill, who stayed calm through
negation, who agreed to bleed some more,
but got so hysterical she ran, tripped,
slip-slid, down, down, slope, scree, sand, taste of salt.

Both myths end up with our kids in the sea.

# Encounters in the Abyss

"Why don't you just swim the whole length of it on
one deep stored breath, you swimming champeen?" yelled
the Animus of the Precipice down to gasping me from on

high, "Faster! Faster!" Me: "Whoa, what good is that? I
aim to Australian crawl, not faster, but smoother, you dumb
Son-of-a-Gun." He: "There! Look!" Me: "What?" He: "Eye!"

He's hopping around up there, and there's no rail. "Bird! Eyeing
your formerly auburn hair for his mate; wait, I see it's
the female of the species so you're in luck! By Jove, I

do believe it's my personal friend, Little-Redtail-Hawk."
I think, right, if my hair's for her, then fine. I shout, "It's okay!"
He's leaning, way over the edge. "Careful, Mr. Life-in-Hock,"

I call, then dive under, and when I surface, I'm named Εὐρώπη.
Gorges lie where continents put them, firm for rivers' later
cascading. Sir Ledge warns, "There aren't outlets in Europe

for the kind of hairdryer you're used to, let alone your flatiron."
Does he think I was born yesterday? I know about adapters.
Besides, I can always use a cast-iron one, the so-called Sad Iron.

I breast-stroke, evoking symmetry, young Eliot in the Alps, yellow
knee-socks in rhythm with his climb, up! up!, his calves
like a yellow butterfly. *Cin-de-rell-a dressed-in-yell-a*

jump-rope-jump-rope-jump-rope-jump-rope *went upstairs*
*to kiss her fella 1 2 3 and~~she's~~buy~~ing~~~a~~~stair~~~~*
*way~~~~ t'heavennnnnnn* Led Zeppelin's vibe in the finale.
Is my Sky God still there? Is my swim done? Am I a finalist?

## Listening Man

He's nothing to me, the listening man
Hearing in Tuscany one mandolin
In chartreuse light from window pairs
Whose arches rise, whose sills run low

Hearing in Tuscany one mandolin
Between a cravat and poised hands
Whose arches rise, whose sills run low
As one man listens, a second man strums

Between a cravat and poised hands
Two girls take turns with reposing eyes
As one man listens, a second man strums
Over napkins of white, two squared to four

Two girls take turns with reposing eyes
Their orbital ridges tinted pink
Over napkins of white, two squared to four
Connecting shadows the purple of plums

Their orbital ridges tinted pink
In chartreuse light from window pairs
Connecting shadows the purple of plums
He's nothing to me, the listening man

# Cornucopia of Arcadia

*Love lives on words, and dies of deeds… The word, which for me
is already the thing, is all I want.*

—Marina Tsvetaeva
(in a letter to Rilke)


*One need not search for the strangest possible things; one cannot
avoid them.*

—Arkady Plotnitsky
(in a footnote)

# I.

For my new job, albeit late-career,
I landed at Purdue pre-tenured, hence
The first meeting I attended was small,
For tenured faculty only, and there
You were. I'd been attracted in advance,
Via your webpage. I was, by contrast,
A complete stranger to you, but, judging
From your face when our eyes locked, a surprise.
I hadn't quite grasped how your bio jibed
With your city's name: Leningrad; née Saint
Petersburg; the reboot, Petersburg. Your
Name I'd pronounced ARK-ady, like "sparkly."
  That first committee meeting, that was when
  I heard. "A body" rhymes with Arkady.

## II.

Fall, when optimism rolls out a grand
Semester, when back-to-school coincides
With Rosh Hashanah, when parking stickers
Are fresh, LOT A, B, C, you and I held
Our first exchange in the lee of a tall
Decked garage. Whom did we know in common?
Allen Grossman. I had just cast off from
A decade marred by work angst and worse love,
Unreturned by one Fred Abrams. Starting
Over, grateful, glad, at campus events,
I'd check where you were in the room, hope for
Chit-chat with you, amidst cheese cubes and grapes
  And seltzer water in clear plastic cups
  And outside *yellow leaves, or none, or few.*

III.

A practiced phony intellectual,
I did not look forward to the moment
You'd see through my disguise. But early on
I was all, oh, Blok, oh, Ahkmatova,
Shkapskaya and who's a good translator,
Like asking a young person where to buy
A good cane. I gobbled anecdotes you
Related: "When _____" (didn't catch the name) "asked
Tolstoy to suggest for anthology,
Ended up with one by Pushkin, one by _____"
(You spoke so very softly) "and six by _____!!"
I said, "Who?" brows up, as in *should I read*. . . .
　　Your hand waving "no, no, he was bumpkin!"
　　But, I was learning: how your laugh sounded.

## IV.

You gave a talk. I asked if you'd send me
The pdf. Print! I punched, ran into
You in the hall, my copy held aloft.
I did not make the mistake of thinking
*Committedly* that the portrait you used
On your cover page was of Sir Isaac;
*Promptly* I was sorry I had blurted
"Newton?" "No, no," you corrected, "Leibniz."
I looked up Newton's face later. Thinner,
Much. Nor were his eyes anything like as
Pleasant-looking as those of your Gottfried
Wilhelm Leibniz. "And anyway," you said,
   "Doesn't matter who it is. Is there for
   Wig." Wig. The wig. The wig? I must have looked. . . .

# V.

Bewildered, me. Why would Leibniz's wig
Be pertinent to your paper? You saw
The need to explicate: "Conference is on
Baroque." Ah. Wig. I said, "Ah. To depict
Coils." You said, "That's right. Curls." You'd misheard me,
Slightly. Trying not to be an inch or
Three taller than you, I leaned back against
The corridor wall. It made no difference:
Coils versus Curls. Both par for the Baroque.
Weeks, allegro. Yet another stilted
Reception, crowd buzz, insignificant
*Blah blah blah* . . . but you let me know something
   Important: ". . . yeah, they use ton of adjuncts
   Yadda yadda *my girlfriend* lives there. Yeah. . . ."

# VI.

International Luminary, you.
*Theory, philosophy, quantum physics.*
Actual genius, actual friendships
With real cognoscenti. Music. Painting.
Mont Blanc! you'd scaled it, studied it at least,
Knew British Romantics, and how to ski
(Hurt knee aside). Postmodernism (that
One also—yep, I snooped—the field of your
Brilliant girlfriend in New York). My moment
Came, however. I simply dropped the mask:
"I've read so little." You said, "That's all right."
Eyes drawn to eyes. I took you at your word,
   Was able to retain my familiars:
   *Milkweed, mud, extra butterfly monarchs.*

# VII.

My mind, maybe call it temperament, saw
Puzzles, not questions. When I mentioned 'I've
Read so little' and you missed not one beat
'That's all right,' I blushed acceptance. That talk
Took place by my desk, where I sat swiveled,
My face toward yours where you stood just inside
The open door. Inside doll's acceptance—
Freedom, and inside doll's freedom—impulse:
To pick up a dried tree-piece I'd brought in,
To say—to you—"branching structure," as though
That modified noun were a whole sentence.
You nodded. And when you did that—my heart
　Grew light: he *gets* me. A man of science
　Taking as equal a wee puzzling lass.

# VIII.

One Friday, I stayed on in my office,
Past darkness at 5:00, past 8:00, past midnight.
Vicious weather outside, soon to be gale.
My windowpanes were chill and opaque, my
Solitude total, my copy of your
Heisenberg chapter unstapled. From it,
I twirled eleven eleven-line odes.
I fabricated axles, repeating
Two eleven-letter words from Shelley
U N R E M I T T I N G I N T E R C H A N G E while the spokes
(I saw them as silver) I extracted
By numerology, a Cabalist,
   One breaking Sabbath, at that. Not merely
   Old—ancient, silent. Sleet hissed on black glass.

# IX.

I titled it "To Gaze at a Wheel with
Eleven Spokes Moving." To be exact,
"To Gaze at a Wheel with Eleven Spokes
Moving: after Arkady Plotnitsky."
Utterly unpublishable. Musty
Pegboard game, frayed cardstock page. I was close
To your age, but older than your girlfriend.
Too old for you? None of that mattered, when
I could scry those ultra-rich surfaces,
*Your Writing*, for patterns. I'd stir without
Altering words, trade lower/upper case,
Impose breaks, watch, emerge, a wedge
   *Of what?*
   *Of nature?*
   *Of mind? Perhaps*
   *Of both, or neither—*
   *Of something else altogether.*

# X.

My poems in your box; your essays in mine.
Do you remember? Once I said, "I put
Kandinsky in there."* You smiled. "I saw that."
After your "Thinking Waves: with Marcelo
Toledo's 'For the Encounter in the
Abyss,'" I used your terms "small mountain lake,"°
I used the title, I used wavy marks.†
Tell me, did anyone back home call you
By endearment "Arkasha"? Your brown eyes,
How they moved me. At night, I played CDs:
Russian all-male a cappella choirs, and
English ballads, the singing of Chris Wood:
   *Oh I wísh / Lord Báteman // yóu / were míne.* Well.
   *And never wás / lóve / só / compléte. . . .* Well. Well.

* see *Beyond the Fire* (Shearsman Books, 2010), pp. 18-19
° see p. 56 in the present volume
† see p. 23 ibid.

## XI.

Your ain true love dedicated her book
*For Arkady*. Acknowledgments, too, serve
As means for sending regards to one's aides
And allies, but as well for declaring
One's devotion. The best are saved for last.
In your many books, she found her name saved
For last. E.g. *for doing everything*
*Possible and a few things beyond the*
*Possible.* E.g. *for her inspiring*
*Presence.* Good for her. Good for love, any
Love. In one of your books, I found my name,
Midrange, an alphabetical list. Five
   Of us, you thanked: *for friendship and shared time*
   *And conversations.* I was thrilled. Thank you.

# XII.

One English ballad told of a local
"Fair maid" and a foreign "bold grenadier,"
Spied "a-making of hay." She sang, *Soldier,*
*Oh soldier, will you marry me?* He sang,
*Oh no, my sweet lady, that never can*
*Be, for I've got a wife at home in my*
*Own countree. Two wives and the Army's too*
*Many for me.* Your mind was too many
For me, Plotnitsky. Brave Gertrude wrote in
"Yet Dish": "Copying Copying it in."
From your work I Copied Copied it in:
*In Monet's cosmos of roses, what may*
  *Be called the* image-gravity . . . *defines*
  *Everything and makes the house disappear.*

## XIII.

With the mental metabolism of
An ant, I could not *really* "read" your work.
I gleaned. I responded in ways I knew
Were not in the dialogue, were only
Idling. You: *There is no decidable,*
*Definitive answer whether there was*
*Something between these two infinities* . . .
Me: (Were roses? was a house? "infinite"?
Yes. Yes. Onward) . . . *contrary to Cantor's*
*Conjecture known* . . . (I loved your phrase "cosmos
Of roses") . . . *known as the continuum*
*Hypothesis* . . . (Your hyphen in "image-
   Gravity" worked for me. Where was I? Aye,
   "Cantor") . . . *that there is nothing in between.*

# XIV.

Where art *interferes*, you'd proposed, *the most*
*Crucial things occur.* Perhaps. Some of those
Years tortoised; some hared. Our manuscript swaps
Flourished, or petered out. Switched off. On. You,
Learnèd: *Have not Shakespeare, Dostoyevsky,*
*Joyce, Kafka, Beckett, or Freud and Nietzsche,*
*If not already Plato and the pre-*
*Socratics, told us as much?* Me, snippy:
*Has not Stein told us as much? that "sugar*
*Is not a vegetable"?* Overall, my
Effort waned. Age spots on my hands waxed. What
To wish, that my spine would last a while yet,
   Or collapse, right away, and finish me?
   Continuum, or crux? I did not know.

# XV.

And yet, what pleasure, just casually
To touch your arm or rather the coat-sleeve
On your arm. Hmm, wool/cashmere blend. Not for
Nothing was I a rag-merchant's daughter.
Alone, I sought margins, without language
But nigh to it. Made X-marks spike. A shoal
Of chevrons. A staircase of Y's. Walls of
Of *of of of of of of of of* of
Sulfur-colored, mustard-colored, clay, writ
Upon by spiders' shadows, not black, but
Brown. I puttered: cogitation without
Proof, urge without lust. I would wash my hands,
 My face, in tepid water, rinse in cool;
 My soap attested to roses and rue.

# XVI.

Fred Abrams, professor, and I, writer
Visiting for the year, bantered. In some
Context long forgotten, I had this line:
"I like fire and knives." He, grinning: "Just when
I'm thinking of having you over for
Dinner." . . . His doorbell, I rang; his door, he
Opened; from behind him came his music:
'Twas Haydn. That was the whole year's zenith.
Nadir? Near meal's end, his dog, Yofi, came
Over to my chair. To pet her, I reached
Out my hand, saw Fred see horror, my fat
Upper arm flap. His eyes flared, *whomp* instant
   Stage-curtain drop. His thought: *No Way*. He could
   Not help that, deserves no rebuke, for that.

# XVII.

As you know, Arkady, I could barely
Read. I couldn't begin to comprehend
Cantor, not to mention beg to differ.
Cantor, there's always *plenty* in between.
"Continuum Hypothesis"? I wrote
*Peat. Now there's a crucial continuum.*‡
Stay alive if you can, I was trying
To say. You need savvy, Horatio.
My philosophy? Put kitchen matches
On the list. Spark/fuel, crisis/gradation.
Still, it may *be* there's nothing "in-between"
Infinities. There was no ground between
   My *Please yes* and Fred Abrams' *Please no*. Two
   Incompatible, rising, endless cries.

‡ See p.57 in the present volume

# XVIII.


Years, I torch-carried, unseen, "friends." He signed
His emails *Yours, Fred.* My book won a prize.
We had fun emailing Re Cover Art.
I did save back one detail, namely that
I had put on the dedication page:
*For Frederick Abrams.* When I snail-mailed him
A copy, he emailed: *Thanks but I don't*
*Deserve it.* Our emails continued. Late
One night, his second paragraph began:
*Beth and I are expecting a child in*
*March.* "Beth" he'd mentioned. Once. Cantor, did I
Regret squandering my page? Yes and no.
  Either your hypothesis was wrong or
  Regrets and pages weren't infinities.

# XIX.

I did not get to be with Fred, and I
Caved in. I did not get to be with you,
And by the way I liked you much better,
But did not cave in. I tolerated
The verge. More than continually, must
Have been continuously, I took my
Chance: dwell, not fall, in love; no pre-defined
Fruition; no feeling of failure of
Feeling, not on either side. At Purdue,
The MFA students are there three years,
Easily long enough for one of them
To break the heart of another of them.
  One young woman broke, that I knew of, two.
  Alas, alack, one was Josh Kaminski's.

## XX.

Josh Kaminski's poems. Mind-startling, funny,
Hurt at heart, smart. Sweet guy, too, who hired on
As department receptionist after
Graduation. I planned on retiring
The next year. Toward you, I wrote (did not send):
*Rich already is my life, and it means.*
*Can it mean Value Added Tax that I'll*
*See you, Double Amphibrach, for the last*
*Time at some staid meeting in Stewart Hall?*
*Will you or will I mind it that nothing,*
*Uh, very much, transpired between us? Come*
*Next blossoms, you might learn, from a listserv*
  *Memo, I'm bending with the remover. . . .*
  Idiot. Did I think I could plan fate?

# XXI.

Serious and in jest, I gave pride of
Place on my desk to a bust, plaster not
Marble more's the pity, of Homer. You
Approved, chuckling. Perfect pitch. You'd observed:
*Human affairs, the main source of philo-*
*Sophical and poetic thinking (al-*
*Though, from the pre-Socratics or indeed*
*Homer on, physics has also served as*
*Such a source)* . . . Carcinoma. Squamous cell.
My tongue. Glossectomy, at least partial.
I said to the doctor referring me
To the surgeon, "I'm in the middle of
   Teaching. Can't I put it off till the end
   Of the semester?" "I wouldn't," he said.

# XXII.

I emailed you re cancer, retirement,
Bending with Atlas Van Lines to move back
Home and would you be willing to adopt
My bust of Homer? Reply: *I'm deeply*
*Saddened to hear this.* I took you at your
Word. A lump in my throat. Another lump
In my throat. You typed: *Of course, happy to*
*Adopt Homer. Just let me know when you'll*
*Be in, or if it's easier, get Josh*
*To deliver it.* Josh with pass-key. Good.
When I knew you weren't in, I nabbed Josh. We
Shlepped Homer. I directed Josh, "Put him
   *There*, so he can see Arkady." Blank-eyed
   Sculpture of a poet famously blind.

## XXIII.

Once more, I glimpsed—you, short, your briefcase large—
Almost like a young boy. I ducked. My poem
Of silver bicycle spokes, I'd revised:
"A Fragment." —*you, aged ten, pedaling fast,*
*Leningrad, among film-like flicker trees-*
*&-shafts-of-brass-light.* One day, you got to
Reminiscing. Soviet Palace of
Youth, your hobby, stamps, "quite nice collection."
I said, "Do you still have it?" "No," you paused,
Long story averted, "No, it was left
Behind." But then, somehow, your pause became—
Mutual. You told me, for all the world
   As if I were your confidante, which stamps
   You specialized in. Fauna and Flora.

# A Carpet Page

Spotted Jewel Weed    White Water Lily    Blue Flag

Shortia Galacifolia    Sabbatia Stellaris    Meadow Lily

Spring Beauty    Oswego Tea    Wild Geranium

Cardinal Flower    Bloodroot    Virginia Cowslip

Indian Pipe    Baby Blue-Eyes    Checkerbloom

Dutchman's-Breeches    Mountain Avens    Chaparral Pea

Tidytips    Black-Eyed Susan    Snow Plant    Yellow Clintonia

Huntsman's-Cup    Fringed Gentian    Saxifraga Jamesii

Pickerel Weed    Butterfly Weed    White Mariposa

California Fuchsia    Creamcups    Southern Red Lily

Purple-Fringed Orchis    Moccasin Flower    Gaywings

Shooting Star    Scarlet Larkspur    Great White Trillium

Orange Milkwort    New England Aster    Prairie Smoke

Purple Prairie Clover    Scarlet Monkey Flower    Gum Plant

Painted Cup    Snow Lily    Rose Mallow    Morningstar

Pentstemon Fruticosus    Bunchberry    Jack-in-the-Pulpit

# A Withy Hut

Возьми на радость из моих ладоней
Немного солнца и немного меда,
Как нам велели пчелы Персефоны.

Осип Мандельштам
(Osip Mandelstam)

*Take some sun and take some honey,*
*simply for joy, straight out of my hands,*
*as Persephone's bees once told us to.*

*(translated by Alistair Noon)*

# P

Peggy married a rich man named Hayden,
but she still comes home each spring. Somebody
has to cope with Mom's depression. The girl's
not pure, nor is it purity she brings.

She brings her smile, which is catching. So Mom,
cheerful once again, resumes advising
the neighbors on land management, if not
against the fallacy that toil outlasts

death. Peggy joins the circular dance that
gives them mirth   *óats / peas béans / and bárley / grów*
In no time flat, it's autumn. Off she goes.
They say they hear her singing 'round the bend

in the road as they hop to Mom's marching
orders. Crops! rotate! ye wheat and ye rye.

## Q

Quaint origin narratives told, Peggy,
alias Persephone, lives real lives,
for one, Margaret's, at 916 Oakbrook
Drive, from which she leaves. Not until after
her daughter and son leave, but she is third.
Last to leave is her steadfast husband, gone

with a surer woman. The house stays put.
It's not on the market. Cracks, angles, gaps,
splotches, cobwebs, birdbath, torn screens. Front, back,
gable ends. Temperatures. Where the closed

garage door meets the driveway, the mold dries,
then pales, then, with fresh rain, inks in its same
green pinnacles. Building and yard, both, seem
to want for her to return so she does.

## Qui

Quietude arrives. On shrubs, snow-mounds glow
within, like opals. Their turquoise valleys
look to her, in hours of watching them not
change, adamant. They, in fact, build up and
waste away. Their summer berries will dot

her sight, the ones at the right height for her.
When ripe enough, these berries are liable
to leave behind, in clay bowls glazed the same
rock-salt gray as her teeth, streaks of near-blue

vermilion. An absence, whose beautiful
face crinkles in the sun, she craves. She has
seen him unclothed, reclining. Nothing shields

her from loss save December's sheer, lambent
scrim. She pines for adulteration. Him.

## She a

She accepts sere July. She may as well
be falling in love. Casings of beetles,

such iridescence, what perfect brooches
for her long black veil. Although no longer
a grower of zinnias, she recollects

zinnias, all the mixed colors, like bridesmaids
from a dozen weddings. She can picture
bracelets, necklaces, shoes, oh and gypsy
sashes to tie around what was her waist

and is now the fold underneath her breasts.
Vines broadcast tendrils, loose threads shimmering
on the breeze. Clover scent visits nostrils.
In ears, which, unlike eyes, cannot be closed,
someone seems to plant shallow sounds, for her.

## She q

She questions what a knife is meant to be.
Like a fish? But slowed down. Must be a dream
knife, then. She still breathes. She lives, not like fish,
in the stream, but close by it, with her kin,
her kith, their cattle. Water to be fetched.

Decay, given time, fells houses, barns, byres.
Lost are dear smells, of stew, of hay, of dung.
Lost is the storybook that made her laugh
to hear the old serving gal claim she was

"born of the Princess of Palestrina
and Pope Urban X." Ninety candles flare
on her cake, many sing, red-rimmed, eyes fill,
her great-grand-nephew blows them out. The knife
skitters in her hand, is taken away.

## She s

She sleeps. Near her sleep tame animals. Not
even old maids with nary a pet sleep
alone. That is because dreams recognize.
Hedgehog. Knife. Hamper. Bunnies. Bunting. She,

no longer desired, inhabits her haunts,
lies on her side, thus enhancing her boobs,
that heaviness, a cloth spread on ground, speed
like unstrung beads, like feathers whooshed skyward,
farther, past the mind behind the Horsehead
Nebula, and back, a small mountain lake.

Come morning, every simultaneous
entity will have slept under and died
out from and woken up to multiple
systems within more than one holiday.

## SI

Sleep, she has learned, is both collective and
private. A Michaelmas sun grows and rots
asters. Plato said that Socrates said,

out of the sense organs, the eye's the one
most "sun-formed." That interesting detail is
not the point. No, the dialogue's about,

obviously, "the good." Let them have it.
That's her opinion. Slumbering, she sees

the hand preserved in the ice by a fluke,
the postcard, the sailor mooring his yacht
in the crevice between mirror and frame.

She seeks fleece, not golden, but clean of burrs.
Peat. Now *there's* a crucial continuum,
soft <—> hard, degrees of dark, how hot it burns.

## St

Striped Muddy Day goes dormant in weary
oxen, unstrapped from the plough, unyoked from
each other. Fresh clods line the tilled-up soil.
Much to come. Sow, wait, harrow, watch, cut, sheave,
load. Mid-harvest, wheresoever farmers
have knocked off for the day, no rain seeming
imminent and knowing how soon dawn is,
they may see fit to leave their wagons out.

Such left wagons tilt into the gloaming,
perpetual. Such tilted rectangles
resemble, but are not, tombstones, forlorn
under high vasty stars. Parallel to,
and cognate with, the planting tracks run lanes,
footpaths for human congress, rights of way.

## The Sun

The sun looks weightless, moves unfettered, weighs
tons, multiple, not manifold. Van Gogh's
pulled-down severed-off left earlobe
must have weighed less than an ounce. The thought of

one ear, manifold not multiple, one
anvil, one hammer, weighs nothing. Van Gogh's
anguish is over with now. High summer,
in the farthest North, sunrise and sunset

can be seen at once, so explorers said.
In the South, only Janus, two-visaged,
a freak, could see time's double cusp. Things, if
manifest, lend themselves to pondering,

especially if they're sad and can't be
changed. Like the cloudiness in Roman glass.

## The Sun's

The sun's a spent coin. She goes to bed.
Her back pain persists. And with her bladder?
Well, she keeps a jar on her nightstand. Lord,

if only, when she cannot get to sleep,
instead of worrying, she'd think over
her good deeds. As a child, times she would share
her bed with a visiting great-aunt, how
she said, "I never sleep with a pillow."

"Really?" said Auntie. "Really," said the girl,
"because then I can stretch my back out flat,"

verisimilitude being a must
to any decent lie. She reconciled, as
necessity, one of the very few
luxuries the poor lady was used to.

## When

When, from profundity, comes up thunder;

when, beneath elaborate costume, hides
the deeply hooded cloak of amnesia;

when dreams dredge up memories too awful
to bear in mind, open-mouthed privation;

when she wakes in disorientation;

when in he rides, the carefree Hidalgo,

a bouquet of radishes to give her,
beans, a dress and a kickshaw, and all on

a sunny afternoon, then of course she'll

bargain, *nunc pro tunc*, now for then, *quid pro
quo*, this for that, tit for tat, how much and

of what kind. Of course she has enough sense

to palm her lantern when dashing in rain.

## Where

Where Spring blows in, not to emptied-out air,
but to seed-conscious air, there her mind fills,
not with death or grief, but with the pattern
of crops, tassels and beards, grainy cosmos.

Where laden boughs stoop to her fingertips,
there she does not hesitate to grasp red.
Where, much later, branches appear to her
as Celtic antlers, there she wears fire-blue.

She employs spin, warp, weft, flaw, cord. From milk,
she skims surface shades of cream, silver tones
from Jersey cows, and from the Guernseys, gold.

For her girl, she decoupages a box
with multiple manifold hands. Design
upon design, in a web, she is free.

## Y

Young and again sandaled, there tall she stands,
unconcealed, half-turns, bends, saunters, tall, done
growing, shadow tall-cast on wildflowers.
Soon, her tallness conjoins nakedness, he
to suffice, herself braced, so that: from then
on, meadow remains her most powerful
metaphor, meadow purring with choices.

She blurs away violence, long past now,
fluid to begin with. Nevertheless,
when she hears, on a single instrument,
melody in a minor key, such as,
from the Irish, "a slow air," then her heart
moves, to revolve around her mother's house,
locus of sorrow, space of vanishing.

# Black Cab Session

This poem is meant to be sung to a setting by Richard Thompson (1949- )
of 'Remember Adam's Fall' by Thomas Ravenscroft (c.1592-1635). Refrains are
Ravenscroft's. See http://www.youtube.com/watch?v=zFx9LIkb3qg

Wood crosses molder soon
Thick lichens blanket tombs
Remember O thou man
Thy time is spent
Wise corbies keep alert
Dominion over earth
Remember God's goodness
Be not afraid


Rain splashed then quick to freeze
Sodden ice-melding feet
Remember O thou man
Thy time is spent
Gorse stiff with pikes of rime
Holds fields till sun can shine
Remember God's goodness
Be not afraid


Hard fighting looms ahead
Ghost women make the beds
Remember O thou man
Thy time is spent
Salt-stained hard-leathern vests
Bold archers next to next
Remember God's goodness
Be not afraid

Castle past closing eyes
Flame-bound and blocking sight
Remember O thou man
Thy time is spent
The thought in amber held
Where light would once up-well
Remember God's goodness
Be not afraid

## An Inland Story

she thinks a name
as if name-thought and touch
were one as the sky
amasses stone-cloud builds
monastery ruins yet ruins
cannot be built
forms effigies who
cannot see yet stare
up into simplified
blue while far below
fencewire rusts
treetops sway
in wind prevailing wind
within which
two horses stand
neck to haunch neck to haunch
two horses
a bay and a roan

# Gardens against the Mower

### 1

I looked a fool, paying Damon
more than he asked for the job of
raking up, my leaves, hauling off,
    my leaves, among which, mid-
        morning
I jumped his bones. When, day done, he'd
planned me no plan, I felt ugly,
    and I felt cheap.

### 2

A hard freeze last night. The boxwood
got burnt. I fret it won't come back.
Not true worry. Just wondering.
    I wish I had less to
        go by,
fewer books, fewer concentric
selves, but one with ruddier skin
    and blacker hair.

### 3

In the retaining wall, one rock
sits loose, juts up. I'm as stuck with
gravity as anyone else,
    out of kilter. Next door,
        Will's pines
thrive, where Damon staked them. And I'm
consoled, recalling Aunt Sara's
    waist-length white hair.

*4*

I wait for, and I engage, mild
sounds from next door, Damon's engines.
Edger. Mower. Blower. I know
    it, absolutely, what
        I hear
when I hear it, that rumbling noise,
his trashcan on its wheels. We both
      know, as adults.


*5*


One afternoon, I smiling said,
"You know, you've never touched my face."
He planted there a right broad kiss
    and grabbed untenderly
        my ass.
I said, "That's not my face." Ha ha,
the quip! ever quick to retrieve
      what I've let slip.


*6*


Will's day on the schedule again.
Since I'm wearing mauve clothes and green
mascara, since I feel my heart's
    fear safe inside these things,
        I could
approach that east window, wave to
my Damon, before he exits,
      before I cease.

7

Will he leave without me? *Oh, yes,*
*oh yes, my dear,* Aunt Sara says.
The hedges. The fences. The walls.
  *Withdraw, it's not too late,*
        *withdraw,*
*shelter from wind, hide from view, deep*
*in the house. Forget. Forget him*
        *now, your Damon.*


8

Through the spring, mowing, long summer
mowing, kisses in the yard, fall
mowing, too. "Call me if you need
    anything," he says. I'm
        standing
here, in the open air, in his
capable arms. Who are we, so
    physically new?

www.ingramcontent.com/pod-product-compliance
Lightning Source LLC
Chambersburg PA
CBHW031934080426
42734CB00007B/690

* 9 7 8 1 8 4 8 6 1 5 8 4 7 *